Written by Beatrice Fontanel
Illustrated by Anne Logvinoff

*Specialist adviser: Dr Jane Mainwaring,
The British Museum (Natural History)*

*ISBN: 1 85103 067 0
First published 1989 in the United Kingdom
by Moonlight Publishing Ltd,
131 Kensington Church Street, London W8
Translated by Sarah Gibson*

© 1988 by Editions Gallimard
English text © *1989 by Moonlight Publishing Ltd,
Typeset in Great Britain by Saxon Printing Ltd., Derby
Printed in Italy by La Editoriale Libraria*

Animals
on the Move

Where have the animals gone,
when it's winter all around?

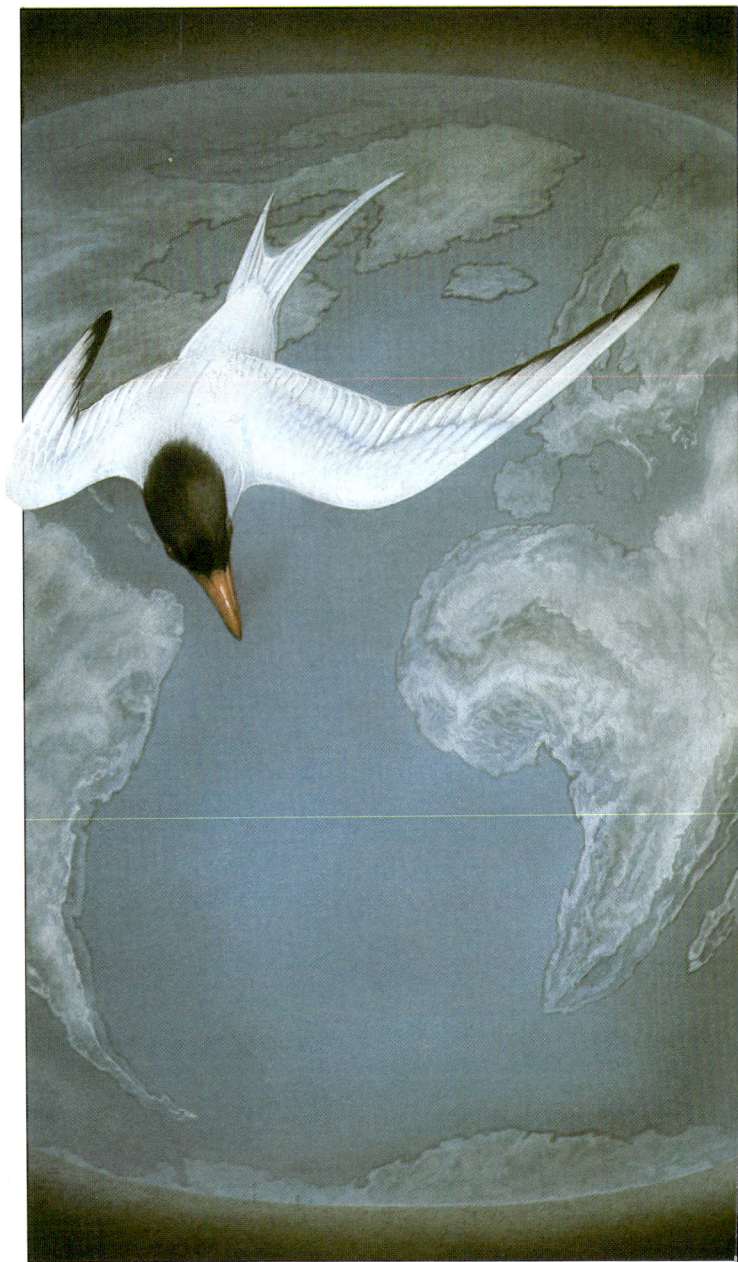

6

Some animals seem to disappear altogether in the winter months. People used to think birds went to sleep in the autumn and did not wake up till spring. Other people thought they spent the winter under the sea, or even flew to the moon!

Today we know that some animals set out on a long and difficult journey to avoid the cold and wet, or to find fresh food. This seasonal journey is called **migration**, and it happens year after year.
But why exactly does it happen?

◄ The arctic tern flies right round the world from one pole to the other.

Geese even manage to fly over the Himalayas, the highest mountains in the world.

Storks spend the winter months in Africa and return to Europe to nest in the spring.

In Alsace, in eastern France, storks nest on the roofs of houses. They come back to the same nests year after year.

In Britain some animals, such as rabbits, sparrows and robins, manage to find enough food in the winter. Others, such as hedgehogs and dormice, sleep in their nests right through till spring. Many of our insects die of the cold. But some of the birds leave to find warmer countries. Such travelling animals are called **migratory animals**.

Why do they bother to migrate? Why not spend the whole year in a hot country? Because in hot countries the summers can be dry and food scarce, but our countryside is overflowing with good things to eat in spring and summer. It is easy for birds to find food quickly for the gaping young mouths in their nests!

One fine day in autumn, you might see a huge cloud of starlings swooping and swirling in the sky, or swans taking off from a lake with a great beating of wings. In the ocean depths, a school of whales is on the move. A shoal of tunny fish hurtles along – even attacks from sharks won't stop it!

What has happened to make these animals gather together to start long and difficult journeys?

The weather is getting colder. The days are growing shorter. Although the animals are well fed and healthy, food is becoming more difficult to find. They feel restless. It's as if a little clock inside them is warning them that it's time to move on . . . and suddenly they're off!

Many sea creatures lay eggs that float freely in the water. The young are carried by currents away from their parents and towards new waters and shores where they settle. This is how new colonies of barnacles, mussels or oysters are formed. Crab and lobster young spend the first part of their lives drifting.

How do fish find their way under the sea?

Most fish have a very good sense of smell. We think that they use a sort of scent map to help them find their way, just as we would use a map with landmarks that tell us where to turn. Some fish migrate when the time comes to breed or lay their eggs. Each year salmon make a special journey back from the sea up to the river of their birth to lay their eggs.

Eels leave their homes in the rivers of Europe to go and lay their eggs thousands of kilometres away in the Gulf of Mexico! There, the surface of the Sargasso Sea is covered with a floating layer of seaweed. The young eels, or larvae, are gradually carried back across the ocean by currents, and as elver enter the rivers and estuaries of Europe.

The young eels change during the course of their journey.

The adult eels do not feed at all while they are migrating.

Turtles live in sheltered bays where they feed on seaweed and grasses. When the time comes to lay her eggs, a turtle sometimes travels 2,000 kilometres or more to find the right hot sandy beach. The turtles that live on the coast of Brazil have to battle against strong sea currents before they reach Ascension Island. There the mother buries her eggs in the sand well above the high-water mark and leaves them to hatch in the sun's warmth.

When snow covers the mountain tops, the ibex move to the valleys for shelter.

Travellers on foot

It is less tiring to move through the air or through water than it is to go on foot or crawling. This is why many birds and fish migrate and not so many land animals do. But some mammals, such as reindeer, do migrate hundreds of kilometres, moving from very cold places in order to find food and to escape the harsh winters.

Even some toads migrate, leaving the forests to look for lakes and rivers where they can lay their eggs.

Travellers on the wing

There are many more travellers in the air…
Dragonflies and butterflies may look
fragile, but some can cover distances of
100 kilometres or more.

Ducks break their journey, coming down for a rest on an
inviting lake or river after a hard day's flight.

Nightingales, swallows, geese, cuckoos,
swifts – these are just a few of the birds
that migrate. Watch for their return to the
countryside, or even to your garden. Which
arrives first? Which tells us that summer's
almost here?

The wood-pigeon leaves the towns and
forests to fly to the Mediterranean lands.

One autumn evening, a bat may set off on a long journey to find a cave somewhere warmer.

Birds travel across whole continents. Their journey may take months.

Hunched on the ground, the pelican is a funny-looking bird. But in the air it is one of the most elegant of gliders.

Many birds return with the same mate to the same nest year after year. The nest is tidied up, the female lays her eggs and a new family is raised.

The black kite leaves Europe early in the summer to return to central or southern Africa.

Look up in the sky at the different patterns made by flocks of birds in flight.

A flight of flamingoes

Birds fly in formation. Ducks, flamingoes and cranes fly in a V shape one behind the other. Sparrows and starlings fly in a cloud. They can follow movement much faster than we can, and so can twist and turn without bumping into one another. When the bird at the front grows tired, another takes its place as the leader.

A flight of sparrows

Some of the smaller birds fly low down, just skimming the earth or the waves. Larger birds, such as pelicans and geese,

fly more than 1,000 metres up in the air. By taking advantage of the air currents that half blow them along they tire less quickly. Swifts even manage to doze off while they're flying along – they just need to flap their wings once in a while to keep flying!

A flight of geese

Do migrating animals ever lose their way?

Not often. They use the sun, the moon and the stars as a guide, just as sailors do.

The Mediterranean Sea is quite a barrier. Birds touch down just before the dangerous crossing and then again on the far shore. They have to gather their strength before the next obstacle – the Sahara Desert!

Sailors use a piece of equipment called a sextant to work out their position from the stars. If it's cloudy and they can't see the stars, sailors use a compass which will always swing to the north.

Birds seem to know naturally just where they are. These sailors of the skies are true navigators. They can alter their direction slightly to make up for the ever-changing course of the stars. Some birds act as though they have an inbuilt compass.

Many birds travel from Europe to spend the winter in Africa. Most of them head off to the east or to the west, so as to avoid crossing the Mediterranean.
1. Black-headed gull   2. Skylark   3. Starling
4. Blackcap   5. Nightingale   6. Cuckoo
7. Hoopoe   8. House-swallow   9. Crane
10. Oriole   11. Fly-catcher   12. Black kite
13. White stork   14. Tern

Greylag geese usually
fly by night and
always very high.

Birds have very good memories. They
are able to remember parts of the
countryside that they have flown over
before. They always use the same valleys,
and follow familiar rivers, coastlines,
crests of hills. Some birds seem to have
learned their route too well. Often they
seem not to know about a short cut that
would save them several hundred
kilometres!

But not every bird is an expert at
navigation. Waders, swifts, ducks and
cuckoos find their way perfectly, but
starlings and wood-pigeons sometimes get
lost. Even if the adult birds manage to get
back on course, the young ones may miss
the route and get lost over the sea.

The eagle is a frightening enemy to a bird weak and exhausted after a long flight.

Migrating animals face great dangers.

Birds may be killed by storms or larger birds of prey. They can also be harmed by any insecticides sprayed over the seeds on which they feed.

A lone caribou that strays away from the herd risks dying in a snow storm.

Many birds follow the River Nile in Africa to avoid the Sahara and its sandstorms. They use the river as a landmark as well as a place to find food and water, but the lights from the traffic confuse them.

Some birds fly as high as 8,000 metres to avoid bad weather but aeroplanes fly at that height too, and sometimes the birds collide with them.

There is danger from the ground as well. Hunters lie in wait for certain kinds of bird that fly past in migrating flocks.

One swallow in two dies during the course of its migration. Those that return in the spring may well have to fight off any sparrows that have set up home in their nests.

Snowy owls catch hundreds of lemmings to feed their young.

Nothing will stand in the way of migrating lemmings. They even lose their fear of humans as they rush through villages.

Wildebeest migrate, following the rains which make the grass grow. Their journey takes them over hundreds of kilometres and through hazardously deep rivers.

Looking for food!

Animals that live in enormous herds must move on in order to find enough food for them all to eat. Only the strongest animals will survive the journey.

When the grass on the plains of Tanzania dries up, wildebeest leave the area in their thousands for the higher wet plains. On the way, most of the young are drowned trying to cross a deep river.

Lemmings live in northern countries. Sometimes too many young are born in one year and there is not enough food to go round. Then they all rush madly to migrate. They won't stop for anything, not even the sea, where many are drowned.

Perhaps one day even the shy springbok will lose its fear of people and let us wander freely through its herds.

A plague of locusts!

Locusts are like large grasshoppers. They live in hot dry countries. If food begins to get scarce, the locusts start to change. First they grow wings, then thousands gather in a gigantic swarm and fly off to find something to eat.

Wherever these voracious feeders settle,
people watch helplessly as their crops are
stripped. There is often no way of
controlling the invasion. The harvest is
spoiled and the people go hungry.

How can we study migrating animals?

First of all, simply by watching them. Notice how they behave. What makes them change their normal habits? Are there fewer in the winter than in the summer?

This pigeon is fitted with a sort of blinkered hood. Will it still be able to tell where it is going?

People have realised that the very same birds they had seen in one country turned up later in another. How did they find their way? Did they use their ears, their eyes or their noses? The only way to find out is to cover first their eyes, then their noses, and then watch to see if the bird behaves differently.

Scientists have observed how birds use currents of warm air to carry them along.

It was always difficult to follow animals that travelled by night. Now radar can record their journeys.

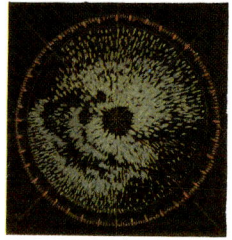

How can we keep track of animals on the move?

Land animals are fitted with collars or studs in their ears which are radio transmitters. Scientists use a special gun to shoot metal tags just under a whale's skin. Minute labels are stuck to an insect's body.

A light metal ring can be fastened round a bird's leg. The ring shows figures and letters, and it won't wear away or get damaged by sea water. If the bird is caught by somebody in another country, the finder will know where it has come from and the date it was last seen.

Bats were caught and ringed in Moscow. Later they were seen more than 1,000 kilometres to the south.

Imagine a bird that could fly from the Earth to the Moon!

That's the distance a swift will have flown during its lifetime if it reaches the age of twenty!

Migration is a very powerful force. From an ant to an arctic tern, an animal on the move can achieve the most amazing feats.

Polar bears trek around the North Pole. The climate there is so harsh that they are forced to keep on the move all the time to find enough food.

The golden plover leaves Canada or Alaska to fly south over the Atlantic Ocean to the far end of the American continent. In the spring, it follows a more westerly route. So twice a year it traces a very precise loop of 12,000 kilometres, and nobody understands why. **Migration is still a mystery.**

The puffin makes a figure of eight above the whole of the Pacific Ocean before getting back to its starting point on the islands off the coast of south Australia.

Index

Now find out about

Crocodiles and Alligators
All About Pigs
Animals in Winter
Bees, Ants and Termites
Wild Life in Towns
Teeth and Fangs
The Long Life and Gentle Ways
of the Elephant
Animals Underground
Big Bears and Little Bears
Wolf!
Cows and Their Cousins
Monkeys and Apes
Big Cats and Little Cats
Animal Colours and Patterns
Prehistoric Animals
Animal Architects
Wildlife Alert!

other 'Animal World' titles
available in the *Pocket Worlds* series

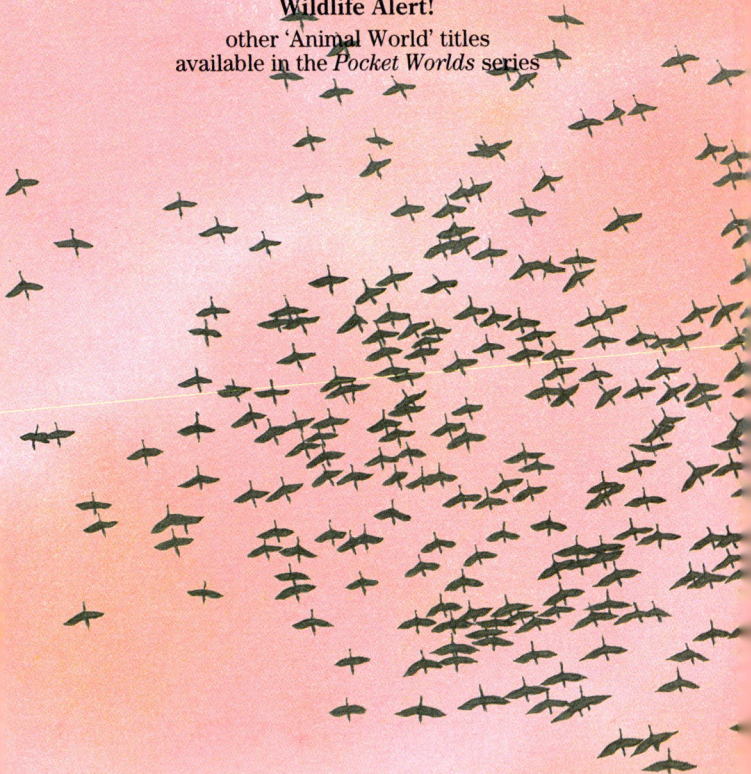